# THE ADORATION OF THE LAMB

# The Adoration
# of the Lamb

PETER SCHMIDT

*Photographs by*
PAUL MAEYAERT

Davidsfonds/Leuven

# Foreword

For a number of man's cultural creations the stock of words of praise in whatever language appears to have been exhausted. One can only expand the list of glorifying terms by means of a continual inflation, whose consequence will be a devaluation of the words and their loss of power. The Adoration of the Lamb retable in Ghent belongs to the category of works of art whose fate this is. Indeed, which overblown epithets still have to be invented in order to describe and appreciate this painting? Though the dictionary may be exhausted of superlatives, the painting itself is not necessarily so. The question will always remain: why is it that a number of masterpieces are so inexhaustible and universal that they remain forever young and are always able to arouse the wonder of the first encounter in all those who come into contact with them - anew, like the birth of every new human? I am thinking of the Iliad and King Lear, the cathedral of Chartres and the Taj Mahal, the St. Matthew's Passion, Don Giovanni, the Sistine Chapel, the Isenheimer Altar... The more familiar one is with these creations, the greater the wonder they elicit.

There will never be a final answer to this question. After all, the reason why a particular work of art always affects and moves generation after generation can never be explained on a purely rational basis. One constant can be found in them all, however: each one of these creations couples the greatest intelligence and mastery of the relevant means of expression with the greatest power to move. The emotions they arouse become stronger and more personal in proportion to the degree to which they are communicated by means of this style, a style that enables the artist's individual emotions to be transposed to the level of universal expression. This allows these works of art to contain a universality that pierces the boundaries of the culture in which they arose and to form a tie between all people. They rise above the narrow confines of their own time or spatial horizons, and touch both the heart and spirit of those who live in another time and place than theirs. At the same time, however, and this is what makes them paradoxical, they are entirely unique. Copied and imitated they may be, but yet unrepeatable and unrepeated. They reflect like a mirror the unmistakable uniqueness of the genius that created them.

The Ghent retable belongs in this class of creation, and in the first rank. Supreme intelligence and technique, emotional power, universality and uniqueness characterize Van Eyck's polyptych and mark it as one of the greatest productions in the history of human culture. During his visit to Ghent in 1521, Albrecht Dürer rightly spoke of the Adoration of the Lamb as "überköstliche, hochverständige Malerei."

A descriptive or explanatory text can never replace the joy and wonder of viewing the work oneself. The spectator should himself discover the breathtaking pictorial richness of this work. Even so, in the following pages we would like to extend a modest hand to help you look, understand and enjoy.

# VAN EYCK AND HIS TIMES

The work of the Van Eyck brothers is unrivalled as a testimony to the magnificent period in which it was produced. At that time, the beginning of the 15th century, Flanders was part of the Duchy of Burgundy and Jan van Eyck's best works were created during the long reign of the Burgundian Pericles: Duke Philip the Good (1396-1419-1467). This splendour-loving monarch provided the stimulus under which Flanders experienced a glorious *Waning of the Middle Ages* (Huizinga), the ripe glow on the eve of the Renaissance, when, however, it would also be impoverished, and prey to devastating religious wars. The Burgundian lands, stretching from the Alps to the North Sea, rivalled France and England in their power and even surpassed them for several decades in their economic prosperity and cultural reputation. Present-day visitors to Dijon and Bruges are still impressed by the many splendid traces of this period of civilization. Many nobles, clerics and wealthy merchants also basked in the glory radiated by the ostentatious Burgundian court. It is for a good reason that paintings and miniatures from that time show a profusion of precious stones and rich garb in expensive, sumptuously furnished interiors. The large Flemish towns were at that time centres of world trade. Not only lords secular and sacred, but also patrician and merchant families that had become wealthy could afford to have renowned artists work for them. Jan Van Eyck's *The Betrothal of the Arnolfini* (National Gallery, London) and Hugo van der Goes' Portinari triptych (Uffizi, Florence) provide perhaps the most well-known evidence of this.

Philip, who had founded the prestigious chivalric Order of the Golden Fleece in 1430, as a reflection of his power and splendour, was also an enthusiastic patron of the arts. Sculptors, carpet weavers, musicians, goldsmiths and many other artistic craftsmen worked under his patronage. But it would be as a Maecenas in the field of painting that Philip was to go down in history, and not least for the very particular association of his name with that of Van Eyck. The duke even became the godfather of one of the sons of Jan Van Eyck, who occupied a position of trust with him.

In the family of painters called Van Eyck we know of three brothers (Hubert, Jan, Lambert) and one sister (Margareta). The family originated in the Maas area in Limburg. Their birthplace is not known with certainty, but the claims of the town of Maaseik, at that time in the County of Loon, are possibly justified, although the area around Venlo is also eligible, and other names have also been mentioned. For further investigation we refer you to the specialist literature.

Hubert and Jan were the most important representatives of the family. Not so much is known about Hubert (Hubrecht) van Eyck. He must have been born between 1360 and 1370 and died in 1426 in Ghent, where his gravestone is preserved in St.Bavo's Abbey[1]. Apart from the Adoration of the Lamb there are no surviving works which can with certainty be attributed to him. His name is, however, mentioned as many as four times in the municipal accounts of Ghent between 1424 and 1426, so one suspects that he was fully active when he died. There is one 'Master Hubertus' known, who in 1409 painted a retable for the Church of Our Lady in Tongeren. The identification of this master with Hubert van Eyck is far from hypothetical. Due to the fame of his younger brother, on whom we have much more information, and upon whom all the attention of the art historians was focused, doubt was later cast on his collaboration on the retable in the Church of St. John, and even on his very existence. Both doubts are considered unjustified at the moment, though it is no longer possible to indicate exactly which parts of the Ghent retable were carried out by Hubert. The design? A number of painted-over sections, such as the grisaille of St. John the Evangelist? Or indeed, as the well-known quatrain on the frame suggests, the greater part of the work? It remains one of the mysteries surrounding the panel. There has, naturally, also been a flood of works written about this question.

The most famous of the two painters by far is Jan van Eyck. He was probably born between 1385 and 1390, and died in Bruges in 1441. Jan was the first Flemish painter to sign his works (nine in all), and eighteen panels can be attributed to him with sufficient certainty. He signed with 'Johannes de Eyck', and on some works one recognizes his motto *Als ich can*. It is as little known as in Hubert's case exactly where he trained as a painter. One detects the influence of Robert Campin, also known as the Master of Flémalle, as well as that, obviously, of the Late Medieval book illuminators such as the Master of Boucicaut and the Van Limburg brothers. The latter worked for the great uncle of Philip the Good, Jean, the Duke of Berry, and produced one of the most renowned books of hours, the *Très Riches Heures du Duc de Berry*.

Jan's exceptional talent, intelligence and character apparently led to his finding great favour with Philip the Good. He became his gentleman-in-waiting, his task being to paint under assignment from the Duke. It was Jan van Eyck, for example, who accompanied a ducal deputation to Portugal to paint the portrait of the Princess Isabella, a candidate for marriage. As confidant he was also entrusted with a number of sensitive and secret diplomatic missions.

We cannot with certainty attribute a single work to Hubert, let alone give dates. As far as Jan is concerned, we only know the works from the last decade of his life. In fact the *Adoration of the Lamb* retable, dated 1432, is the oldest dated composition by the two masters. It was at the same time a 'masterstroke'. It was with the Van Eycks that the world-famous 15th-century school of painting, later to be called the 'Flemish Primitives', made its start. This school has enriched the world with a number of extraordinary masterpieces. To mention only the most famous of the artists, in the wake of Van Eyck: Rogier van der Weyden, Dieric Bouts, Hans Memling, Hugo van der Goes.

It is therefore hard to overestimate the importance and influence of the Van Eycks. To quote E. Dhanens: "The power of their imagination has long made a great impression, as has the then totally new, faithful rendition of visible realities, the significant meaning of the representations and the technical perfection of its execution, by which means the colours have kept their qualities with an unsurpassed brilliance."[2] It was due to the exceptional quality of the work and material that the legend came about that the Van Eyck brothers had invented oil paint. This is not the case, but the *Adoration of the Lamb* and Jan's works display sufficiently well by which giant steps they advanced the then still new technique of oil painting.

Van Eyck's influence on later masters was indeed enormous, praise of the exceptionally high level of their work has remained unanimous from the start, and since the 15th century the accumulated studies and analyses would now fill a library. Our purpose is much more modest. It is our intention to provide a short and practical historical, thematic and aesthetic introduction to their greatest creation: the *Adoration of the Lamb* retable in St.Bavo's Cathedral in Ghent.

# THE RETABLE AND ITS HISTORY

We find a very important piece of information about the history of the retable, phrased in rather awkward Latin, in the quatrain painted onto the lower frames of the outer panels:

> Pictor Hubertus e Eyck major quo nemo repertus
> incepit pondusque Johannes arte secundus
> (frater) perfecit Judoci Vijd prece fretus
> VersU seXta MaI Vos CoLLoCat aCta tUerI.

Translated fairly freely, this means: "The painter Hubert van Eyck - none greater has ever been found - commenced (this work), and his brother Jan - the second in the art - completed the weighty task, at the request of Judocus Vijd. With this verse he places what has been produced under your guardianship (or: so that you may look at it)."

The last line of the verse contains a chronogram of the year 1432. In other words, the verse offers a deal of interesting information: the retable was unveiled on 6th May 1432. Hubert van Eyck started it and Jan completed it after Hubert's death in 1426. It was commissioned by Judocus Vijd [3].

Like most of the important Medieval works of art, the *Adoration of the Lamb* was the fruit of a commission and delivery. At that time it was the custom for certain groups (the guilds) or wealthy individuals (rulers, well-off burghers) to make gifts to a church or a monastery for the production of a monument or a retable, for example, by which means they wished to maintain a particular religious practice. It was also common for them to be portrayed on these works of art as the donor. A number of these gifts served as a visible mark of a 'foundation', which means that people gave money in order to help 'found' a devotional act - mostly a mass, which was to be performed at predetermined times. This also provided the occasion for the painting of the *Adoration of the Lamb*.

Judocus (=Joos) Vijd, Master of Pamele, was a prominent citizen of the city of Ghent. He belonged to a rich family of financiers and was married to Isabella, who was from the well-known Borluut line in Ghent [4]. He was an alderman several times and from 1433-34 even *voorscepene*, which corresponds to what was later called the mayor, and therefore belonged among the main figures on Ghent city council.

Joos Vijd was part of the parish of St. John, and on one occasion paid for the repair of one of the parish church's apse chapels. This is the chapel which is today still called the 'Vijd chapel', the second chapel to the right of the middle radiating chapel or sacramental chapel, situated in the southern choir aisle [5].

For this occasion it was his, and his wife's, wish to have a retable made, to perpetuate a foundation: a daily mass "to the honour of God, His divine mother and all His saints", and intended for their heavenly bliss and that of their ancestors.

It is thought that he commissioned the work from Hubert in about 1420. It may, however, have been earlier. It is no longer possible to say exactly what Hubert's share was in the making of the work or in what way it is to be distinguished from that of Jan. Research into the brush technique, for example, has provided no definite answer to the distinction between the two different hands. It seems logical, however, to ascribe at least the concept and composition of the work to the elder brother, as well as the first stages of its execution. But it is also impossible to determine with any certainty whether, or to what degree, changes were later made to the concept. There have been writers who would ascribe very little or almost nothing of the present retable to Hubert. Other, more recent, specialists prefer to consider Hubert as responsible for the greater part of the retable. This conclusion is drawn from, among other things, the fact that it would otherwise be difficult to understand the praise of Hubert (in the quatrain) as the greatest of painters, and the supposition that Jan was not able to work for long on the painting. After all, from 1425 on, Jan was continually occupied with assignments for Philip the Good. He was probably only able to work on the retable after 1430, with the permission of the Duke. It is on this assumption that it is thought that Jan finished off the work, that he made a few alterations to the composition, introduced changes to the Annunciation panels on the closed section - Jan is thought to have been responsible for the present interior of the room - and finally that he painted the portraits of the donors and also Adam and Eve entirely. But in this hypothesis, Hubert could have been responsible for most of the inner section. An indication of the share painted by the two masters may lie in their different approaches to the organization of space. Hubert is thought to have worked fairly flatly - for example, in the panels with the angels singing and playing music, and the three central figures; Jan, on the other hand, is thought to have introduced more depth - in the Annunciation scene, for example. Our short introduction to the retable does not allow us to go any deeper into this complex debate. From now on we shall consider the polyptych in its final state, as an integral work, painted by both Van Eyck brothers.

The retable was closed on ordinary days. It was opened on Sundays and religious holidays, and it drew crowds of people to the Church of St.John from the very beginning. The retable fulfilled its liturgical purpose up to the end of the Ancien Régime, and it remained in the chapel for which it was painted, and which determined the rendering of light and shadow, until only a few years ago: the Vijd Chapel.

Face to face with the exceptionally well-preserved polyptych in St.Bavo's today, one might think that it had remained undisturbed in its original position for more than five centuries. The reality is in fact entirely different. The retable has had a remarkably eventful history, and it can only cause amazement that it can today still be admired in such complete and perfect condition. We shall pick a few important dates and events from the past centuries.

The St. John's church board took great care of the polyptych, so that the first thorough cleaning of 'Joos Vijds Taeffele' only took place in 1550, carried out by the painters Lancelot Blondeel and Jan van Scorel. Before then, a predella in watercolour ('De Helle') had already been erased by incompetent painters. Marcus van Vaernewijck accused them of having worked with the 'hands of a calf'... During the religious riots of 1566 and 1578, the polyptych was removed from the Vijd Chapel twice, in order to preserve it from destruction. In 1662-3 the work was cleaned again, and on that occasion was also mounted on a new Baroque altar. It underwent a restoration in 1731.

During the period of the French Revolution, in 1794, the four central panels (3,4,5,10; see plan) were taken to Paris. It was only after the Battle of Waterloo (1815) that they were returned to Ghent. Shortly after this, in 1816, in the absence of De Broglie, the Bishop of Ghent, the side sections, six panels (2,6,8, 9,11,12) without Adam and Eve, were sold by the 'Grand Vicar' Le Surre to an art dealer in Brussels. Having been sold on to the English collector E. Solly they ended up in 1821 in the possession of Frideric William III, King of Prussia, on display in the Berlin museum. It was there that the quatrain on the frame of the outer sections was discovered. In 1894 the panels were sawn through in section and laminated for display purposes.

In 1822 the middle panel showing the adoration of the Lamb split horizontally, caused by the moving of the retable to save it from falling ash during a fire in the cathedral. It was possible to save and restore it, however. In 1825 the panel with the Holy Virgin was restored by the painter Lorent. In 1861 Adam and Eve were transferred to a museum in Brussels in a transaction with the Belgian state. By that time the parts of the retable were entirely separated from each other. In Ghent the remaining original parts were complemented with copies by Michaël Coxcie (1559) and Victor Lagye (1865). Lagye clothed Adam and Eve with animal skins, and these clothed copies can still be viewed at the rear of the cathedral as curious evidence of a rather Victorian mentality.

In 1914, when the First World War broke out, the four remaining middle panels were put in safe storage, and were returned in 1918. In the Treaty of Versailles it was laid down that the Germans were to return the six panels in Berlin. They were first brought to Brussels. The complete retable was reconstituted in Brussels and exhibited, then brought back to Ghent. In 1920, after more than a century, the retable was again complete and could be admired in its original position.

In 1934, on the night of the 10th of April, one of the panels sawn through in Berlin was stolen. On the outside it shows St. John the Baptist and on the inside the Just Judges. The thief (or the fence) signed with the initials D.U.A. the letters he sent to the Diocesan authorities demanding ransom money. Despite dozens of theories, the meaning of these letters has still not been deciphered today. In order to prove that the panels were in his possession, D.U.A. gave back the grisaille with St. John, placing it in the depository at the North Station in Brussels, while keeping the panel with the Just Judges hidden. Although it is thought that the name of the thief or fence - Arsène Goedertier from Wetteren, a borough in East Flanders - had been known since his sudden death in November 1934, the panel has remained untraceable despite many searches. In the place of the stolen panel there is now a successful modern copy by J. van der Veken (1939-1940), a painter who had also attended to the Adam and Eve panels in 1936-7.

There have, naturally, been countless hypotheses and studies put forward concerning the theft of the Just Judges, from the extremely serious and meticulous to the completely fantastic. It is in any case a theft that appeals to the imagination, and the mystery surrounding it is supplied from time to time with freshly-spiced nourishment. Diviners, clairvoyants, Templars, Rosicrucians, they will all be found on the search-path. The sober and realistic detection of the panel is already eventful enough for those who don't want to let their imagination run away with them. Its progress has brought with it a lot of creditable detective work, but also errors, mistakes and unexpected turns, and really positive results have not yet been achieved. In Ghent, the whole business has become an unsolved romantic thriller, which keeps on agitating a number of minds. But will the original ever again see the light of day?

In 1940, on the outbreak of the Second World War, the retable was taken to Pau, in the Pyrenees, and hidden there in the castle of Henry IV. In 1942, however, the German occupiers (who also searched for the stolen section in Ghent) took it away to the castle of Neuschwanstein in Bavaria, and in 1944 it ended up in a salt mine in Alt Aussee in Austria. It was discovered there at the last moment in May 1945 and saved from imminent destruction, together with seven thousand other art treasures. It came back to its original place in Ghent via Munich and Brussels. During 1950 and '51 the painting was thoroughly examined, restored and treated for conservation.

For the time being, the last important date in the history of the retable was the year 1986: for reasons of security and conservation and after long discussions, the retable was taken from its original position in the Vijd Chapel, and on 11th July was transferred to the specially reinforced and converted baptismal chapel (the so-called 'Villa Chapel'), at the rear of the cathedral. At the same time the retable was set up for display in a bullet-proof case and remains permanently open. Although measures definitely had to be taken for the security of the priceless work - only in 1978 the St.John the Baptist panel was damaged by a fall - the transfer to the baptismal chapel remains a much contested interference. Apart from the fact that the retable can no longer be stolen, the slight colouring inherent in thick protective glass and the lack of viewing distance for the outer sections are considered by many to be annoying.

# EXPLANATION OF THE TERM 'THE ADORATION OF THE LAMB'

The polyptych in the cathedral in Ghent bears the title 'the Adoration of the Lamb of God'. It's certainly true that the subject of the central panel is the adoration of the Lamb. Many contemporary admirers of the retable come from other cultural backgrounds than that of Christendom, and therefore it will be useful to provide a few words of explanation regarding the subject and its depiction.

In the central panel we can see a lamb standing on an altar. It has been slaughtered: blood is pouring from a wound in its chest and this is collected in a chalice. There is a halo in the shape of a cross around the lamb's head.

The Lamb of God is a symbol for Jesus Christ. The Christian faith avows that Jesus Christ is the Messiah, God and man, who saved sinful mankind by means of his crucifixion and resurrection. He is the mediator between God and man, who has opened the gate to eternal life. His words and example have also shown everyone the way to enter the 'Kingdom of Heaven' through love and justice.

The representation of Jesus Christ as a Lamb comes directly from the New Testament [6]. More specifically, it is the writer of the Book of Revelation that is reponsible for the development of this symbolism. The great 'Vision of the Lamb' begins like this in the book: "And between the throne and the four living creatures and among the elders, *I saw a Lamb standing, as though it had been slain...*" (Rev 5,6). The whole of the heavenly liturgy of the Revelation then unfolds around this Lamb. The fact that it has been slaughtered refers to Christ's crucifixion; that it is standing refers to the Resurrection. Christ is alive.

Christ is also denoted by means of this symbolic image in the Gospel of St.John. St.John the Baptist pointed him out to his pupils with the words: "See the Lamb of God".

It is not easy to demonstrate the precise significance of the connection of the symbol of the Lamb with Christ. The fact is that various themes interweave, all of them most probably taken from the Hebrew Bible, the Old Testament. The following are the foremost symbolic elements:

The image of the Lamb of God may refer to the Jewish *Paschal Lamb*. The ritual of the old Passover (Pesach), in which a lamb is eaten, is described in the Bible. See Exodus 12, where Moses provides precise instructions for the celebration. The eating of the paschal lamb is linked to the commemoration of the flight out of Egypt: the children of Israel were liberated from slavery and led to the Promised Land. Jesus was crucified during the Passover celebrations in Jerusalem, and in accordance with an important tradition, his 'Last Supper', his farewell meal with his pupils, was a Passover meal. In any case, the Christians very early on linked the crucifixion of Christ with Passover. Christ, who freed the world from the slavery of sin and death by means of his crucifixion, was therefore associated with the symbol of the paschal lamb. The paschal lamb, which is at the same time a symbol for the Communion meal, is indeed represented on a great many Christian altars and communion rails. [7]

A second symbolic element is to be found in the prophetic books of the Old Testament. The prophet Jeremiah compares himself to an *unsuspecting lamb being led to the slaughter* (Jer 11,19). This prophet, who had to endure a lot in the way of hostility and persecution, is often seen by the Christian tradition as a premonition of Christ. The motif is even more clear in Isaiah 53. In a poem, the prophet evokes the form of the chosen 'servant of the Lord', who will suffer for the well-being of the people: "Surely he has borne our griefs and carried our sorrows... But he was wounded for our transgressions, he was bruised for our iniquities... He was oppressed and he was afflicted, yet he opened not his mouth, *like a lamb that is led to the slaughter...*". From the very beginning the Christians very obviously applied this text of Isaiah's to Christ, who had given his life for theirs.

A third and final motif does not originate in the symbolism of the Lamb, but in the ritual of the 'scapegoat' on the Day of Atonement, Yom Kippur. This ritual is described in the 16th chapter of the book of Leviticus. In a solemn liturgical act the priest lays his hand on the the head of a goat, while he confesses his own

sins and those of the people. This 'scapegoat' is then sent away into the desert under escort, and 'carries away the sins of the people'. The theme of the scapegoat, that carries away the people's sins, has been transferred to the Lamb in Christian tradition. At every Communion the prayer goes: "Lamb of God, that carries away the sins of the world…". The link between the two motifs must be sought in the opening words of the communion at the Last Supper, when Christ says that his blood will be shed for the sins of the people. These words are still repeated at the high point of every Eucharist, the consecration: "this is my blood, which is shed for you and all people."

The Deliverance of the Passover, innocent and vicarious suffering, the carrying away of sin: these are the most important areas of meaning in the symbolism of the Lamb of God.

# WORKING METHOD, CHARACTERISTICS, AND GENERAL APPRECIATION OF THE WORK

Art historians have already confirmed in every way and very emphatically that the golden age of Late-Medieval Flemish painting started with the *Adoration of the Lamb*. This is indeed hard to doubt. The work is and remains one of the all-time triumphs of painting. No one can remain unmoved when face to face with its magnificent symmetrical composition, exuding a sublime calm, and with the overwhelming intensity of the colours. Those who know nothing of painting are struck dumb, but even the greatest connoisseur of art - not to mention the creative artist - can never entirely possess the secret of its beauty. Van Eyck has the rare gift of offering aesthetic emotion and joy to both simple spectators and the greatest specialists, each on their own level.

Perhaps it is not entirely pointless to mention that, for its period, this was an exceptionally large work. Its 25 m² of painted surface represents about 85% of the total surface area, ever painted by Van Eyck, of which we are still aware. This means that all other existing works by Van Eyck together amount to hardly one fifth of the Adoration of the Lamb. At a time when large areas were only painted in fresco, and the other painting techniques were usually limited to book illumination, portraits and, in particular, much smaller retables, the format of the Adoration of the Lamb must have struck the people enormously, and contributed in no small degree to Van Eyck's reputation. In 1432 the time of the giant canvasses of the Baroque and later was still a long way off!

As far as the artists' working method is concerned, we cannot convey it better than by quoting from the superb booklet by A.L.Dierick: "The retable of the Adoration of the Lamb was painted on oak. Several planks had to be joined for the larger panels, which at later stages sometimes led to the damaging of the work. The wood was carefully sanded smooth and coated several times with an emulsion of chalk powder in glue, a coating that when dry was as hard as stone and completely disguised the grain of the wood. The surface on which was painted can best be compared to glossy white ivory. After preliminary drawing, one coat of paint after another was applied, using fine brushes. These coats of paint consisted of a drying oil in which very limited quantities of grains of pigment were dissolved. This type of paint coating, called a glaze, hardens like e-namel and retains a high degree of transparency; light penetrates it and reflects off the white undercoat: it is as though a source of soft light shone through the painting. For this reason no reproduction can do full justice to the real thing: they can only act as a stimulus to go and view the original." [8]

*The painter is amusing himself with a collection of unusual headgear. The Book of Revelation has a crowd 'from all races and peoples and tongues' approaching the throne of the Lamb. The universality of John's vision is here fulfilled, but without words. This motif provides the artist with a reason to play like a child with colours and shapes.*

*Creation of perspective and transition from light to shadow. It is surprising how much depth the tiled floors give to the rather flat panels of singing and musical angels. At the same time the floors provide an interesting example of the discrete way Van Eyck intersperses the retable with texts intended to explain its meaning. We see two sorts of tiles. The first sort displays a regularly-repeated pattern of stylized leaves and flowers in quadruple. On the other tiles there are motifs, monograms and sigla concerning the subject of the retable. The Lamb, standing with the standard of the cross, sign of the triumph of the resurrected Christ. IHS, the monogram of Jesus (the artist or restorer made a slight mistake on the panel with the singing angels, where we can read IHB on one of the tiles; a Gothic S and B do in fact resemble each other).*

The astonishing freshness with which the colours of the Adoration of the Lamb still shine has for centuries prompted questions about 'the secret of Van Eyck'. The extraordinary way in which the linseed-oil paint is handled, has, as already mentioned, led to the story that Van Eyck had invented the technique of oil painting. This legend has been kept in existence by the erroneous interpretation of a story by the Italian writer Giorgio Vasari in his book *The lives of the most celebrated Italian architects, painters and sculptors* (1550). Before oil paint came into fashion, painting was done with tempera. That means that the pigment was mixed with water and egg-white. The colours were more matt, and craquelure appeared sooner. The oil-painting technique, which gives a much greater depth and glow to the colours, was not invented by Van Eyck, to be sure, but he did perfect it to an exceptional quality and manipulability. His panels do not become darker, nor do they yellow or crack. The exact way he worked with oil paints remained a mystery until recently. In the nineteen nineties Pim Brinkman, the art historian from Leyden, and Evert Thielen, a painter, have done a number of interesting experiments, and it is now considered that the solution has been found: Van Eyck mixed boiled linseed oil with lead and applied this as a first insulating coat over the undercoat of filler. This coating was not absorbed by the layer of filler, but remained on the surface as a film. This procedure meant that the colours of the paint itself were not absorbed into the undercoat either, and the painter was able to achieve the uncommon glow which they still radiate today. In addition to this, Van Eyck also used egg-white in emulsion in the paint, and turpentine as a diluent. [9]

Andrea De Kegel writes, correctly: "Hubrecht and Jan van Eyck's contribution to the art of painting was of exceptional significance, both in the field of techniques and that of artistic notions, which were fundamentally changed in the early 15th century by both artists. They carried out a considerable improvement in the application of oil-painting techniques. Their paintwork took on a marvellous glow, produced by the application of various coats of transparent paint on top of each other. In addition to this they broke away drastically from

the exclusively decorative use of colour. By the introduction of intermediate tones and the softening of the gradations from light to shadow, they strengthened the modelling, the volume and the space. The Van Eycks also discovered that colour tints in nature are determined by the material from which the objects are made and the degree to which they are lit. They understood that the further the object is from the eye, the lower the intensity of its colours. In this way they succeeded in carrying the feeling of space, such an essential element in the reproduction of nature, into the art of painting. All these new findings, which are illustrated copiously in the Adoration of the Lamb, form a compendium of knowledge that took the art of painting a decisive step forward." [10]

From the historical point of view, the Adoration of the Lamb is a document of its time, providing abundant information about the Burgundian culture. House interior and architecture, the rich bourgeois and regal clothing and the liturgical robes, headwear, weaponry, musical instruments.. It seems like an imaginary museum of objects from the time of the Burgundians. In fact the whole retable breathes the spirit of the circles in which the Van Eycks moved: the wealthy middle-class and royal courts. The world of the humble, poor and insignificant is far off in this glorification of Christ. Art clearly has a different ethos.

The Adoration of the Lamb, however, is also a pictorial synthesis, and that is much more important. It comprises a summary of painting genres. One can see the study of the human body and the art of portraiture; landscape and cityscape painting; group compositions; grisaille, architectural painting, perspective and trompe-l'oeil, the study of volumes and three-dimensionality, and so on.

One can debate endlessly the question of whether the Ghent retable signifies an end or a beginning. The discussion can be compared to that concerning Johann Sebastian Bach. Bach cannot be counted among the revolutionary musical pioneers, in contrast with someone like Arnold Schönberg. Bach's work is,

*The Greek letters Alpha (A) and Omega (Ω), which in the Book of Revelation denote Christ as beginning and end. The Gothic M for Mary. In addition there is the rather puzzling inscription AGLA, which we most probably should decipher as the initials of a Hebrew formula: Attha Gibbor Leolam Adonaj - 'You are strong in eternity, Lord'. We find the same inscription on the horizontal band of the red cross that runs across the shield of one of the Knights of Christ. There is also a letter-motif that's hard to read, in which some people read the name VEYCK. A signature?*

The lifeless objects bring life to the scene. Van Eyck grasps the paradoxical strength of still-life exactly. The effect resulting from the entry of light is also remarkable. Every point of light and shadow in the entire retable is tuned to the light entering through the stained-glass window of the Vijd Chapel where it originally stood. Even the marble column in the window in panel 18 receives light from this angle, despite the sky outside. There is just one exception: in the small room behind Mary the sun shines on the wall and through the carafe on the window-sill, in the opposite direction to that in every other part of the retable.

In the future, in Renaissance Italy, Piero della Francesca was to go much further in experimenting with different angles of light in one composition (The Chastisement of Christ). But the delicate play of light in the Adoration of the Lamb also reveals the demands and freedom of this genius of painting.

rather, a synthesis of all existing musical genres (except opera), which he brought to a peak of perfection and expressive possibilities unknown until then. After Bach the fugue had no more to say, unless it were to take a radically new direction. In this sense Bach brought a period to a close. But his genius is so unique, his synthesis so masterly, that they were to exercise an enormous influence and precisely by this means brought about new developments, even though it was by virtue of the fact that he brought a period to an end, and forced the creativity of those who followed - starting with his own sons - into other directions. The situation regarding the Adoration of the Lamb is to a certain extent comparable. The work is a synthesis of the medieval Gothic styles of the region. It is not really possible to go any further in the same direction. But it is precisely the way Van Eyck surpasses and perfects all previous achievements that also makes him an innovator. It is the nature of the genius that makes it new, and no one could see reality in the same way again after Van Eyck.

In various ways the altarpiece seems to signal the transition from a Late-Gothic perception of the world to the atmosphere of the Renaissance. Compared to older retables, the Adoration of the Lamb marks a clear advance in the study of perspective and three-dimensionality. This can be seen in several panels: the background to Mary and the angel in the Annunciation scene; the washbasin; the floors on the open section; the landscape which, although its horizon is rather too high, still foreshadows the distant views to come; the groups of saints... The interest in nature, which appears scientific, is also reminiscent of the Renaissance. The trouble taken, for example, in reproducing, exactly and identifiably, 42 sorts of plant [11] comes from a range of interest different from that of the religious Middle Ages. An approach like this leads to an association with Leonardo Da Vinci. It looks as if Van Eyck was already approaching his surroundings with an empirical interest. Perhaps the term 'Renaissance' makes us think too much of Italy. This is not really our intention. It's not necessary to foist any particularly Italian influences on Van Eyck. Nor is his mentality that of the Italian rage for innovation. It may not be forgotten that 13th and 14th-century Western Europe had already known Roger Bacon and William of Ockham, who had prepared the way for empiricism, and that the dawn of humanism was already glowing in the universities in Van Eyck's time.

One of Van Eyck's most astounding abilities was the reproduction of materials. Whether he was painting gold brocade or worsted, wood or crystal, pearls and precious stones, a copper pot and candlestick, the tin organ pipes, the shining harnesses on horses in their tackle, flowers and herbs or crumbling rocks, the artist staggers the spectator with so much skill. Van Eyck displays such a passion for reality that it reminds us of the pointlessness of so many unseen details on sculptures and choir stalls in the late-medieval cathedrals. Which spectator will notice, for example, that the artist has painted the reflection of the whole of the Vijd Chapel window in the sapphire decorating the clasp on the cloak of the foremost singing angel (panel 2)? It is only by using modern means of enlargement that this detail has come to light. Who will testify to the meticulous attention with which the play of light was painted on the half-full glass carafe on the window sill in the room behind Mary in the Annunciation? We are here still a world away from the theatrical outlook of the Baroque, which would often not even finish off the back of a sculpture because the spectator was never supposed to see it. Van Eyck's attention is devoted not only to what he wants to show. He has the pure fascination for what exists and what he himself sees.

The Adoration of the Lamb is thoroughly 'earthly', infinitely more than Fra Angelico or Memling, for example. By this I mean not so much the atmosphere of abundant opulence that pervades the retable - the epithet 'ethereal' cannot be applied to the Adoration of the Lamb! - as the fact that the work of art reveals an avid interest in the world around us - the world of here and now. This aspect, in all its Gothic style, is also already pointing to the atmosphere of the coming Renaissance. The passion for what the senses perceive is carried to extremes. In this sense the work is highly sensuous, and that is why it is great art. It demands the greatest painting skill to allow the spirit and the soul to speak through the matter itself. Many paintings remain below the level of sensuous reality and therefore become bogged down in superficial observation, though they may be technically perfect and true to nature. Van Eyck sees the building, the bush, the washbasin, the velvet tassel... He is enchanted by it and he possesses the skill to express its soul. In his case one understands that there is no other way of expressing the soul than through the material itself. Van Eyck also sees man in this world, and studies and respects his physicality. This attention paid to man brings him once more into the proximity of the Renaissance.

The masters of the Adoration of the Lamb possess not merely the virtuoso ability of the illustrator, who reproduces things 'just like the real thing'. However incredible their technical virtuosity is, the Van Eycks do not illustrate. There is much more involved. Spectators looking at the Adoration of the Lamb are strangely enough overcome by a reverence and even a shudder of awe for the materials themselves. The spectator is affected by the mystery of the contemplation. Van Eyck does not contemplate the exterior of his materials. It is as if he removes the surface on which the eye rests and exposes its depths, so

*Nothing escapes Van Eyck's attentive gaze. The sapphire in the cloak clasp reflects, by refraction, the whole frame of the stained-glass window opposite in the Vijd Chapel.*

*The depiction of fabric and the volume of the velvet tassels with the golden cross is exceptionally fine. The pictorial arrangement is again masterly: a red tassel exactly in the middle of the deep-green background formed by the cloth. The cross: a glowing ember, a spark of light that lends even more depth to the shadows.*

that one encounters the essence of the material. In this way his art rises above a purely photographic documentary realism, just as that of Johannes Vermeer would, two centuries later, in a completely different yet similar way. The concrete object is not an end in itself. Like all great visual artists Van Eyck is also a master of abstraction. But paradoxically enough, you might say that the painter who achieves abstraction does so, not by withdrawing from materiality, but on the contrary, by immersing himself in it and extracting its inner essence from below the surface. It is precisely his unprecedented closeness to the concrete reality that creates the distance necessary for understanding. The Cartesian division between the ego and the expansive world cannot be found here. There is none of the Kantian duality between *Ding an sich* and *Ding für mich*. It is as if Van Eyck - unconsciously ? - succeeds in showing the 'an sich' of what appears to the eye as a phenomenon. There is nowhere one can discover with greater truth

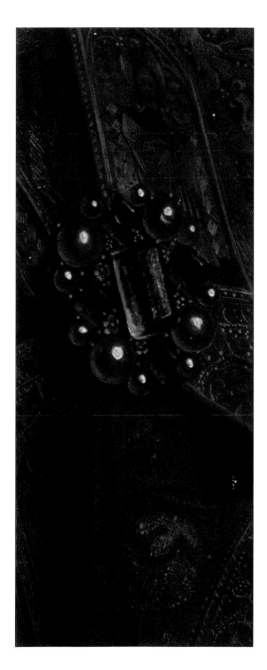

# THE POLYPTYCH'S
# ICONOGRAPHIC CONTENT
## *General*

The iconographic content of the Ghent retable is unique. By this we mean: it does not appear in any other paintings in this form. This should be clearly understood. Of course we come across virtually all the themes dealt with elsewhere in medieval painting and sculpture: the representations of Christ, Mary and John the Baptist; the Annunciation; prophets, saints, donors etc... Van Eyck was not inventing anything here, but was drawing on Christian tradition and on an existing repertoire of figures and types. His painting is unique in the way these different motifs are interpreted and combined into a whole. It can be compared to the unique content of Michelangelo's Sistine Chapel. The combination of religious motifs demonstrates such a richness and diversity that there has been doubt about the original unity of the concept. And indeed, one might question the connection between the upper figures populating the open retable and the large scene surrounding the Lamb below. Not only is the scale of the figures very different, but the characters in the upper section appear not to be concerned with the events below. Even so, this last may probably be primarily attributed to the undramatic and juxtapositional style of painting, and the unity of concept remains defensible even after all the questions. What is worth noting is that Van Eyck did not paint his retable in a narrative style - like a story in serial form - which was very common in our regions in the Middle Ages, but that he returned to the static expression we come across in Romanesque and even more so in Byzantine art. Van Eyck is averse to any form of the anecdotal.

The work's highly original composition is due to various factors, a number of which will probably never be discovered. Van Eyck's symbolism does not limit itself to those themes generally used and understood by everyone, but comes across as complex, difficult and, for the contemporary spectator, even occasionally obscure. Yet the polyptych contains a surprising number of explanatory texts, both on the painted area and on the frames. They are mostly Latin texts, either as an inscription or on a banderole, which are intended to explain the significance of figures and scenes. The texts were applied with such calligraphic skill and so well integrated into the whole that they are very inconspicuous - see, for example, the inscriptions on the backs of the thrones.

The themes should in any case be understood in terms of the liturgical purpose of the retable, that is, the daily celebration of a sacred mass 'to the honour of God, His blessed mother and all His saints' [12]. According to the Catholic rites, every celebration of mass or communion is a commemoration of Christ's sacrifice, by which means sinful man was redeemed. This used to be formu-

Perfection does not exist in this world. All artists, even when their name is Van Eyck, are only human, and sometimes have to correct their work. Here are three well-known 'repentirs' from the Adoration of the Lamb. One of the organist's fingers was adapted to the musical chord. The line of the foremost strap on the harness was changed. And two earlier ears remain on the Lamb. Note the blood dripping onto the altar cloth between the Lamb's front legs. Another example of observation.

lated as follows: Christ's bloody (historical) sacrifice on the cross is brought up to the present day in the Holy Communion in a bloodless (sacramental) way. This commemorative notion, central to Christian belief, may be the simplest unifying factor in the retable. The crucifixion of Christ itself is not depicted. It is as if in this respect one is referred to what is taking place on the altar during the mass. The central scene, however, is the adoration of the slaughtered Lamb, symbol of Christ, surrounded by the instruments of Jesus' Passion and death, and in this way the mystery of the cross is not absent from the actual scene. When, in 1458, on the entry of Philip the Good into Ghent, the rhetoricians acted out the Adoration of the Lamb in a *tableau vivant* in the Poel, it was interpreted as *Chorus beatorum in sacrificium Agni Paschalis*, which means more or less 'Chorus of the blessed for the sacrifice of the paschal lamb.' We point out that the theme of the Lamb may also have been inspired by parochial considerations. The Lamb is after all also the symbol of John the Baptist, patron saint of the then St.John's Church. John the Baptist is portrayed twice on the retable. The Lamb of God is his symbol because it was he, John the Baptist, who, according to the fourth gospel, designated Christ by this name to his pupils (John 1,36).

There is no need to doubt that the painters - perhaps in the first place Hubert? - allowed themselves to be guided in their iconography by one or more theological sources of inspiration. The astonishing wealth and complexity of thematic connections indicates this. Perhaps the priest at St.John's at the time, the learned master Johannes Van Impe, played a part as a mentor. The principal source of iconography was obviously the Bible. But others were the commentaries by ancient Fathers of the Church and medieval theologians. One thinks first of all of Rupert of Deutz and his elaborate allegories.[13] But the allegorical reading of the Scripture was a characteristic of both the Fathers of the Church and the medieval figures. We may assume that the Adoration of the Lamb contains a treasure house of symbolic and allegorical references which are probably not all clear to us anymore. This fact should advise us to be cautious in the interpretation of the individual scenes. It has, for example, often been said that the positioning of Adam's right foot contains a reference to his expulsion from paradise. Such interpretations are difficult to disprove, but they can take the spectator boundless distances into allegory, even into all kinds of esoteric theories, and in this way blind him to the essentials.

The retable also undoubtedly served a catechismal purpose: the explanation and presentation of certain information regarding the faith, for the people who came to pray before the retable. The abundance of texts points in this direction. Though one must take account of the fact that the texts themselves were illegible and incomprehensible to the ordinary people. They are full of abbreviations and some of them still remain obscure. As an exegesis of the retable they can only have provided direct help for scholars and experts.

The retable primarily depicts the glorification of pious mankind, in a representation taken from both the Scriptures - especially the Book of Revelation - and the liturgy of All Saints. A text from the seventh chapter of Revelation is read in the All Saints liturgy. It describes the gathering of all the chosen ones before the throne of the Lamb: 144,000 chosen from the 12 tribes of Israel, and in addition 'countless masses from all races and tribes and peoples and tongues'.

The wealth and variety of diverse scenes connected to this central theme, however, makes this retable also suitable for the evocation of other parts of the church liturgy. The announcement of Christ's birth on the closed section may refer either to the related festival in the church calendar or to Christmas. The whole of the Easter period (the resurrection and exaltation of Christ) with the Passion (Christ's suffering and death) is evoked in the central panel. Other themes present are Whitsun (the Holy Ghost) and possibly the Trinity. And finally, the remembrance of angels, saints and martyrs, so important in the Middle Ages, is to be associated with the retable. But all the motifs used in the current composition of the work are intended to depict the whole mystery of the redemption. We shall now follow this in the individual scenes.

# Short summary of the images

THE OPEN POLYPTYCH

1. Adam; 1B: the Sacrifice of Cain and Abel.
2. Singing angels.
3. Mary, queen of heaven.
4. Christ exalted on the Throne (or God?).
5. John the Baptist, Forerunner of Christ.
6. Angels playing Music.
7. Eve; 7B: Cain's fratricide of Abel.
8. The Just Judges (copy).
9. Christ's Knights.
10. The Adoration of the Lamb of God. Groups A to F.
11. The Hermits.
12. The Pilgrims.

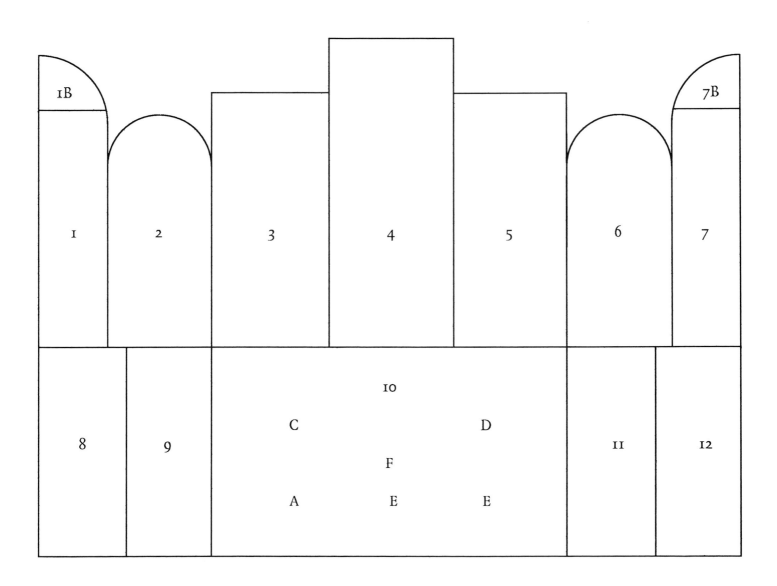

## UPPER LEVEL
One might summarize this section as the 'heavenly court', flanked by the ancestors of mankind, Adam and Eve.

### Panels 1 and 7
On panels 1 and 7 we see, placed symmetrically with regard to each other, Adam and Eve. According to the Bible they are the ancestors of the whole of mankind and also committed the first sin of disobedience to God. The Biblical myth tells how they were banished from the Garden of Eden as a result of their sin, and had to go to live in a land of hardship and misery, where sin grew ever more rampant. Christian theology has always linked the figures of Adam and Eve to its doctrine of the 'original sin'. But coupled to this original sin we find the motif of God's plan for the salvation of mankind through His son Jesus Christ. In this sense Adam and Eve are in the perfect position: it is with them that mankind's tragic history of sin commences, but the deliverance of mankind is also set in motion by their *felix culpa*. Neither let us forget that in the Christian tradition Jesus Christ is called the 'new Adam', the one who nullified everything the first Adam (Adam = man) had brought about, and set the bliss of forgiveness and eternal life against the curse of sin and death.

Neither of these figures stands among the crowds below, but rather above, on the same level as the heavenly ones. Yet the background is not heavenly blue, in contrast with all the other panels on the open retable. They are standing in a niche, from which Adam appears to be stepping forward. The detail in the foot that extends over the edge is a clever specimen of perspective painting, which brings out markedly the three-dimensionality of the figure. Our ancestors are presented with the symbols that remind us of the Fall: they cover their nakedness with fig leaves. This reminds us of the Bible story, which tells us how Adam and Eve realized their nakedness after the sin and made aprons for themselves out of fig leaves. Eve is, moreover, holding in her hand the 'forbidden fruit' that also stems from the famous Bible story (Genesis 2 and 3). Note that the fruit in this retable is not the traditional apple. Nor is this stated anywhere in the Bible. In this painting Eve is holding an etrog, an oriental citrus fruit, in her hand. As far as is known this is a unique depiction in Western art, but it does correspond to rabbinical traditions concerning the forbidden fruit. The etrog is the citrus fruit used in the Jewish Feast of Tabernacles. This remarkable fact may indicate that Van Eyck was in contact with Jewish Bible scholars for the development of his iconography. [15]

It also appears from the writing on the frame that the painter wishes to refer to the Fall: *Adam nos i[n] morte[m] praecipat* - 'Adam casts us into death' and *Eva occidendo obfuit* - 'Eve caused harm by killing'. The attitude of the two figures is not dramatic or tormented, however, as it is in Masaccio's work in the Brancacci chapel in Florence, or in Michelangelo's in the Sistine Chapel in Rome. They are represented with the same sublime calm as the other figures in the retable. Both our ancestors gaze into an indeterminate distance, with a look that exudes inner contemplation and serenity. It is as though they can already descry the ultimate salvation of their descendants. By Renaissance standards their anatomy is not entirely correct, but the two heads are executed superbly. Adam in particular radiates an impressive presence. Note that Adam has points of light in his eyes whereas Eve does not, entirely in accordance with the notional light entering through the window of the Vijd Chapel opposite.

The figures of Adam and Eve were linked on a pictorial and thematic basis to the other panels by the picture on the wooden lectern in panel 2. It depicts the combat between Archangel Michael and the dragon, a traditional representation that refers to the victory of heaven over sin and the devil, which at that time people had already seen foretold in the Bible's tale of paradise (Gen 3,15).

The first consequences of the sin are depicted in the two small quarter circles above the names Adam and Eve: the offer of Adam's first sons Cain and Abel (A) and the consequent fratricide by Cain of Abel (B). Here too the iconography follows the Bible story in Genesis 4. At the same time a reference to the death of Christ was already able to be made here, the murdered Abel providing a preview. The figures are represented as sculptures, making up part of the upper arches of the niches, which are also painted as if in sandstone.

*Panels 2 and 6*
The panels 2 and 6, also positioned opposite each other in perfect symmetry, show singing and music-making denizens of heaven. They are traditionally designated as angels, though a little doubt creeps in here, since they are shown without wings. Compare them to the other angels in the retable ! Angels or saints, it is not of great importance. The figures are painted in a compact group, flatter and tighter in composition than Adam and Eve. The heads emerge from a flat, bluish-white background suggesting heaven, but without much spatial effect. More depth is projected by the floor laid in sumptuous glazed tiles, which disappears into the background behind the figures. Apart from various monograms, one also sees the triumphant Lamb of God depicted on the floor.

These panels have been praised for centuries. What is certainly striking is the marvellous reproduction of material things, both in the heavy, shiny brocade, the embellishments ('aurifrisiae') of the robes and in the jewels, the wooden Gothic lectern, the organ, the chair and the musical instruments. Van Eyck gives free rein to his astonished, attentively examining gaze, sensual in the purest sense of the word, which exposes the very soul of the material. The pitch of the singers' voices can also be made out from their facial expressions. The spectator, however, as we mentioned above, should not let himself be diverted too much by this trueness to life. For that matter, the faces of the musicians are not highly individualized. They seem, rather, to belong to the same

facial type, somewhat smooth, sexless and without much personality. The relationship between colour and surfaces that Van Eyck created is of a more profound beauty. To give a few examples: How masterfully the sharp green triangle of the edge of the cope, folded down, determines the division of areas on the singing angels panel, creating a balance between the red of the cope and the brown of the lectern ! On the other section the metallic sheen continues from the organ pipes through the organist's brocade to the bronze chair-legs; this dispersal of light determines the whole panel's especial luminosity. This, and other pictorial motifs like it, bring the spectator much closer to the reasons behind the greatness of the painting than he would appreciate from its trueness to life alone. Van Eyck does not imitate reality. He creates and presents it. In his own way, he creates, pictorially, an abstract reality in colour and surface just as much as Paul Klee and Picasso would much later.

Panel 2 represents a small singing *schola*. Eight voices singing polyphonically in pairs. On panel 6 we see the instrumentalists, with a small harp and a viola, grouped round the incredibly beautifully reproduced positive organ. The opulent magnificence of the seated figure of the organist (an angel? Cecilia ?) leaves no one unmoved. Apart from this, there is a striking resemblance between Van Eyck's instrumentalists and the ensembles from the period of the Burgundians and Flemish Polyphony, as found in manuscript illuminations and on wallhangings.

*Panels 3,4 and 5*
The three central panels, 3,4 and 5 dominate the polyptych and establish a special pictorial connection with the lower sections by the use of red, blue and green. One can trace the ubiquitous, discrete presence of this relationship when, for example, one looks at the three red corners of the imaginary triangle formed by the central figure of God above, the figure dressed in red, below

left, and the figures attired in red robes, below right, in the middle panel. The red antependium on the altar in the meadow, made obvious by the white ellipse formed by the Lamb and the angels, reinforces this colour composition with four red points of focus. Red/blue/green actually dominates the whole colour climate of the open retable in many subtle and at first apparently inconspicuous combinations. Notice, for example, the way the green of the meadow in the middle plays a part in linking the symmetrical setting of the blue cloak of one of the Just Judges on the left to Christopher's red robe on the far right. Or look at the subtle contrast between the red sleeve and the green cloth under the book against Mary's blue cloak. It cannot escape the attentive spectator that the red/blue/green interplay in the three figures in the foreground of the bottom left-hand corner of panel 10 form a sort of discreet echo of the three main figures in the upper section. Links of this sort need not always be composed along rational lines. But even if they came about spontaneously and irrationally, they still determine the brilliant unity of a great work of art. This precision is what one calls natural talent.

Many gallons of ink have been used on the presentation of the three main figures themselves, especially the middle figure. The figures of Mary (3) and John the Baptist (5) are unambiguously identifiable, but there are still dogged discussions about the middle figure. Is it God the Father, or Christ, or a combination of the two? In this modest guide it is impossible to go into the debate. But we shall summarize a few of the arguments.

There were a large number of motifs in Byzantine and medieval iconography to which painters were very closely bound. One of them is the so-called *Deësis*, a Greek word meaning 'supplication, intercession'. It was a fixed motif which was to be found on its own but also, and primarily, in depictions of the Last Judgment: Christ, passing judg-

*Polyphony and echo in colours. A theme is repeated elsewhere in the work, slightly altered. When we print both groups the same size it is striking what a strong pictorial link there is.*

ment, is flanked by Mary and John the Baptist, who plead for mercy for the sinners. Countless icons depict this subject, but a clear Western example can be seen in the famous Last Judgement by Rogier van de Weyden in the Hôtel Dieu in Beaune. There is a Last Judgement in the Municipal Museum in Diest, painted in 1413 by Lieven van den Clite and destined for the Castle of the Counts. It very clearly shows a *deësis* group and is therefore an important witness to the presence of the motif in Ghent before Van Eyck's time. The *deësis* group is often extended by means of angels, apostles and prophets. So a representation of Christ on the throne, with Mary and John the Baptist, is normally a *deësis*. It is quite probable, therefore, that Van Eyck, who was undoubtedly acquainted with Byzantine and Gothic retables, let himself be guided by the motif of the *deësis*. In his case, however, we are not dealing with a real Last Judgment (even

though there once was a predella with hell or purgatory at the foot of the retable), and neither do Mary and John take on pleading poses. John the Baptist is pointing at the central figure and this is a clear argument for the latter being Christ. The embroidery on the brocade tapestry of honour behind the figure contains, stitched in gold, a motif that traditionally refers to Christ. It is a pelican which, according to old popular belief, tears open its breast to feed its young on its own blood. The motif, encountered in numerous pictures, is a clear and generally well-known symbol of Christ, who gave his blood for his people. In addition there is, above the pelican, a banderole with the words "IHESUS XRS", and the whole motif is surrounded by vine branches, another eucharistic symbol for Christ. The sceptre and the crown at his feet may also point to Christ's kingship. It is said of the Messiah in the Bible that 'his sceptre

*On the retable it is discrete and inconspicuous - but it's there! With connections like this a great talent creates unity in a work whose many sections and variety of scales and representations might have made a disparate impression.*

*Van Eyck again achieves the perfect marriage between the impressive depiction of materials and a powerful element of pictorial abstraction: the fabric of the brocade is regal, but equally it is a column of red and gold between two antithetically placed green triangles.*

*Van Eyck teaches a lesson in painstaking trueness to life as a channel for geometric abstraction probably nowhere better than in the deservedly famous organ pipes. The perfect reproduction of the material become a play of lines in grey and white. Fifteenth-century realism and yet radically modern.*

will not yield' [16]: he is, after all, *Rex regum et dominus dominantium* - king of kings and ruler of rulers. There is a text from the Book of Revelation that concerns Christ, and which may have served as part of the inspiration for the portrayal of the figure on the throne. : "...He wears *many diadems on his head... He is wrapped in a cloak baptized in blood. And his name is: God's Word... And on his cloak and on his thigh a name is written: King of kings and Lord of lords*" (Rev 19, 12-16). This last title, in Latin, can be read on the bottom hem of the cloak, in letters made of pearls stitched to the hem.

Nevertheless, a number of motifs argue in favour of God the father. First of all there is the motif that possibly has to do with the Trinity. When the retable is regarded as a whole, there's a straight line that runs from the Lamb, through the dove, to the middle figure at the top. The Lamb undoubtedly represents Christ, the dove the Holy Ghost. One might then think that it was logical to identify the uppermost figure with God the Father, because then we have a representation of the Trinity: Father, Son and Holy Ghost. On the oblique golden band crossing the robe we see the word *Sabaoth* (with the Greek omega). This Hebrew word that means 'hosts', is part of the combination *Dominus Deus Sabaoth* - The Lord, the God of Hosts. This title often appears in the Old Testament, and is therefore in Christendom also normally reserved for God the Father. That is certainly the way it works in the text of the *Sanctus* in the Catholic mass. The text of the Sanctus is taken from a vision of the prophet Isaiah, in which the Seraphim call out: 'Holy, holy, holy, is the Lord of Hosts' [17]. The beginning of the text on the golden throne may also point in that direction: *Hic e[st] Deus pote[n]tissim[us] p[ro]p[ter] divina[m] maiestate[m]* - This is God, all-powerful because of his divine majesty etc...' In addition, the papal tiara is usually a symbol of the Father rather than the Son. And there is also the motif of the Revelation: He who sits upon the throne (Rev 4,2; 7,15; 20,11; 21,5; 22,4 et al.). Normally one also reads God the Father in this figure. In Rev 5,13 the song of praise of the creatures goes: "To Him who sits upon the throne and to the Lamb be blessing and honour and glory and might for ever and ever." So He who sits upon the throne

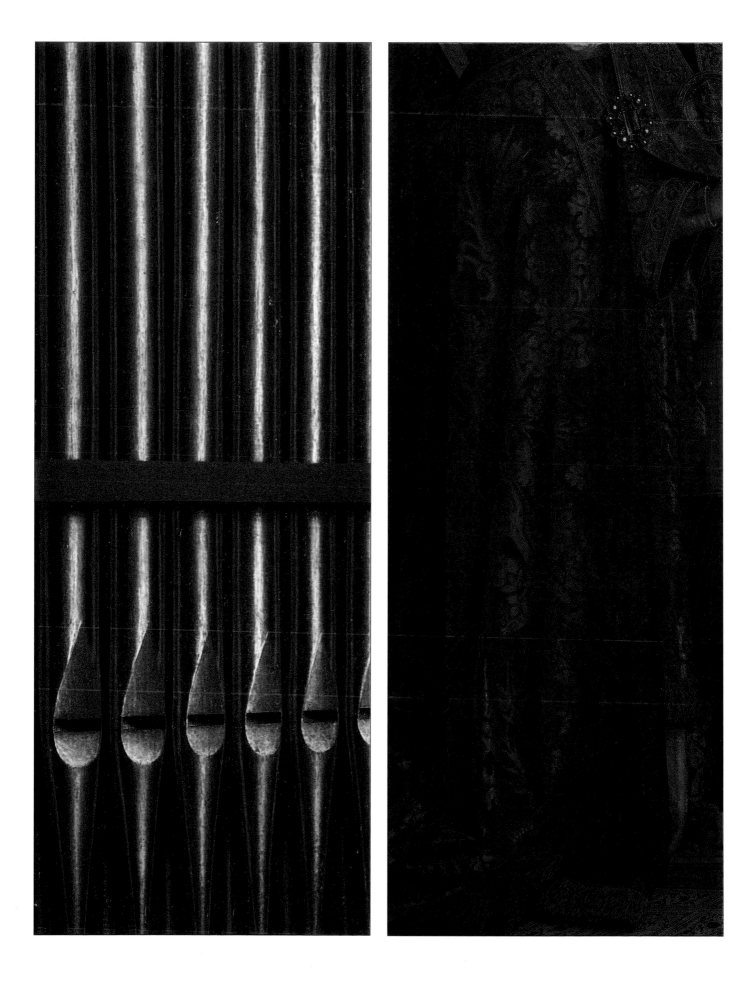

is clearly distinguished from the Lamb. On the other hand the great liberties taken in the use of such references make it hard to find compelling arguments.

It is not easy to cut the knot. Considering the dogma of divine equality between Christ and the Father, it is always possible that a number of titles and symbols of God the Father are transferred to Christ. This has happened often in Christian tradition, in particular the symbols concerning dominion and omnipotence. Symbols typical of Christ, however, such as the pelican, were never normally transferred to the Father. That's why we tend more in the direction of identifying the figure as a glorified Christ. But this does not entirely solve the controversy. A number of Van Eyck connoisseurs are of the opinion that a conscious combination of the two has been sought, a sort of fusion of characteristics, in order to suggest the unity of Father and son. [18]

With a calm gesture of blessing and a sceptre, the figure dominates the whole event. He is represented rigidly from the front, impassively hieratic, as in both Byzantine and Romanesque art. His shoes, painted almost vertically, like a Byzantine emperor, rest on a step in front of which lies a golden crown, in open work with acanthus leaves. Is this to indicate his own regal might, or does it symbolize his power over all dominions? Does the artist want to say that spiritual authority (tiara) is higher than worldly authority (king's crown)? Or that both belong to Christ? Questions like this are hard to answer. The painter has reproduced the scarlet robes and all the embellishments with an exceptional technical expertise. The representation of the crystal sceptre alone is an event in the history of painting. It is in the treatment of the figure of Christ that we see how meticulously Van Eyck exploits the illusion of the light entering the Vijd chapel: every fold in the cloak, every pearl and precious stone, however small, receives light and shadow from the window opposite. All the accessories and decorations, such as the pearls on the hem of the robe, the tiara set with precious stones, the crown and the clasp of the cloak, also unsurpassedly express divine, transcendent majesty. We may undoubtedly read into the whole representation a variation on the well-known iconographic theme of the Pantocrator, the 'Almighty'.

To Christ's right (left for the spectator) Mary is enthroned. *H[a]ec e[st] speciosior sole* - this woman is more beautiful than the sun, says the inscription on her throne. The blue of her cloak is created by pigment made from lapis lazuli, and is the bane of all photographers. Reproduction of this colour is almost impossible. Mary, a ripe young woman, does not plead and does not even look up to Christ. She is absorbed in the reading of a breviary. Calm, peace, serenity, inwardness, these are the terms that come spontaneously to mind when looking at this picture. The exquisite face, set in a soft waterfall of hair, stands out against the background of the throne. The pale-blue background of the tapestry of honour, embroidered in gold, forms the transition between the dark-blue robe and the yellow of the throne. The diadem is decorated with roses and lilies, symbols of Mary, and the twelve stars remind us of the woman in the Book of Revelation: "And a great portent appeared in the sky, a woman clothed with the sun, with the moon under her feet, and on her head a crown of twelve stars" (Rev 12, 1). Van Eyck left out the apocalyptic painting of sun and moon, but in-

*How should one characterize this representation? Expressionless? Without feeling? Über alle Gipfeln ist Ruh? The rigid emotionless frontality of the Pantocrator, with its absence of any trace of drama, shows better than any other panel how far distant Van Eyck is from the romantic ideal of art as 'most personal expression of the most personal emotion'. However different the style may be, the face of the Godly figure can yet summon up associations, both with the rigidity and sublimity of a Byzantine mosaic or icon and with the 'serene emptiness' of the face of a Buddha. There is something strange about this calm impassivity. There is no contact with the spectator. It appears to be the expression of a perfection which, in its reflection, is sufficient unto itself. Is this coolness? Some people will certainly experience it as such. Is it mysticism, rising above the unsettled and changing times? The image itself seems to radiate that of which it is the object: the eternal unmovable calm of the beatific vision. In any case, this Almighty exudes a spirit that's imparted to the entire retable.*

tegrated the circular glittering of stars perfectly into his portrayal of the queen of heaven. Once again one discovers the incomparable subtlety of the play of colours: red, blue and green, in the diadem and against the dress. The golden band running through the deep blue; the floor, which deepens all the colours and links the three figures together.

John the Baptist is the third figure in the deësis. Over his camel-hair prophet's tunic he wears a green cloak bordered with precious stones, sign of the glory in which he is included. But his bare feet remind us of the ascetic life of the desert dweller. John raises his index finger towards Christ. He is the forerunner of the Messiah, and indicates his coming. The representation of John the Baptist pointing at Christ reminds one, among other things, of the passage in St. John's Gospel in which John the Baptist points Jesus out to his pupils. "The next day John was there again, now with two of his pupils. He turned his gaze on Jesus, who was passing, and said: look, the Lamb of God." [19] It is hard to think of anything more applicable to the Ghent retable.

John is also holding a book on his knee, its red leather clasp straps contrasting superbly with the green cloak. Compare this pictorial element with the contrast between the green tiara ribbons hanging down on Christ's red cloak: green on red for Christ, red on green for John: a connective contrast! The book is open at the first page of the prophecy of Deutero-Isaiah [20]. This prophecy begins with the word *Consolamini* - 'Comfort, comfort my people', and heralds the voice crying in the desert to prepare the way of the Lord. This prophecy is put in John the Baptist's mouth at the beginning of the gospels, in order to prepare for the coming of Christ. One can read the word *Consolamini* on the book. Notice also how the prophet's beige-brown belt creates a colour transition between the creamy white of the pages of the book and the brown of the prophet's cloak. The genius of Van Eyck's play of colours can also be seen in the tapestry of honour on John's throne: the narrow space between the golden embroidery is… coloured green.

We would like to point out a striking characteristic of the figures in the upper section: they do not show any involvement with each other. Adam and Eve look neither at each other nor at any other particular figure. The angels also appear to be playing music for themselves, and the three central figures are, as it were, also caught up in their own worlds. Their gazes do not meet, there is a diffident division between each of them. This is an element that plays a part in the striking absence of human passion and dramatic or subjective involvement in the retable. This is not an expression of individualism or egotism, however, but the ultimate transcending of the individual to the universal. I cannot do better than to compare it to Rublov's icon of the Trinity or the music of Bach. In this extended objectification of the event the timeless serenity of eternity emerges unadulterated. It is precisely because the figures do not impose any feelings or mood of their own that they leave the spectator entirely free, and direct him to the essence.

*The panel 10*

The five panels (8-12) of the lower section give a greater impression of unity than the separate figures above. We have to start with panel 10, the large central scene from which the retable takes its name, the Adoration of the Lamb. Groups of people are coming forward from all sides round the Lamb of God. They are flocking towards the heavenly liturgy, and the whole thing is undoubtedly inspired by the scene in the Book of Revelation: "After this I looked, and behold, a great multitude which no man could number, from every nation, from all tribes and peoples and tongues, standing before the throne and before the Lamb, clothed in white robes, with palm branches in their hands..." (Rev 7,9). There is no text that could describe the festival of All Saints better. But Van Eyck never simply illustrates texts. He is, once more, not an illustrator. For example, he will give the robes different colours and not give everyone a palm branch. But the texts provide the inspiration for his subjects, which he then handles and transforms with the freedom of an image-maker of genius.

The heavenly liturgy takes place round the divine Lamb on a rolling meadow lined with fruit trees, bushes and flowers.

The attention has often, and rightly, been drawn to the staggeringly rich variations in green contained in this fairly closed landscape with a rather high horizon line. As a background this green provides all other colours with a warmth of their own. Even the affectionate eye of the researcher and the technical perfection with which the individual plants are reproduced are frequently praised.

   Pictorially speaking, above all else the attention is drawn to the white Lamb on the altar with the white altar-cloth and red antependium. Lamb, cloth and angels' robes form a white ellipse that draws all attention to the central scene (F). It is here that the liturgical purpose of the retable is clearly revealed: the altar refers to the daily Eucharist, and the representation of the Lamb to what, according to Catholic theology, takes place on the altar. It stands on a rise, which may symbolize Mount Sion in the heavenly Jerusalem (Rev 14, 1). The Lamb has been slaughtered and blood flows from its breast into the chalice. The reference to Rev 5,6, 'The Lamb, as though it had been slain...' is clear. The chalice, which receives the blood, obviously refers to the wine in the communion, Christ's blood. The words of the consecration are: "This is the chalice with my blood, shed for everyone". Gathered round the altar kneel 14 angels. Four of them, at the rear, bear the instruments of Christ's Passion. We can distinguish, from left to right: cross and crown of thorns; nails and spear; pole with sponge soaked in sour wine and scourge; whipping post and rod (or reed stem ?). Again a clear reference to the significance of the Lamb on the altar. Two angels at the front, one of them bearing wings like a closed peacock's tail, honour the Lamb with incense. This also contains a reference to the honouring of the communion flesh and blood of Christ. The writing on the antependium leaves no doubt, and involves the the spectator in the events of the communion: on the upper frame we read *Ecce agnus Dei qui tollit peccata mundi* - 'see the Lamb of God that takes away the sins of the world', a formula which is spoken or sung

before the communion in every Eucharist. On both the cloths hanging from it we read: *Ihes via, v[er]ita[s], vita* - 'Jesus is the way, the truth and the life'.

In the middle foreground there is a fountain (E). Twelve fine jets of water splash into an octagonal basin, flowing from ten dragon's heads round a ringed, bronze column, and from two phials carried by an angel on the column. The crystal-clear water flows out from the base of the basin into an encircling channel whose bed is strewn with precious stones, and then rushes away into a stream that passes out of the painting in the foreground. The religious symbolism of the fountain takes many forms. The painter himself gives an indication: on the edge of the basin, which appears to be in Italian marble, are the words *Hic est fons aqu[a]e vit[a]e procedens de sede Dei + Agni* - 'this is the source of living water, springing from the throne of God and the Lamb'. This makes reference to both the Book of Revelation and to St.John's Gospel. In the vision of the heavenly Jerusalem, at the end of the book of Revelation, the writer has depicted a vision taken from the prophet Ezechiel, which goes as follows: 'Then the angel showed me the river of the water of life, as clear as crystal, surging up at the throne of God and the Lamb...' (Rev 22, 1). On the bank of this river stand the trees of life - a reminder of the Adam and Eve paradise story - that bear fruit twelve times a year and provide the people with cures [21]. May one think of these trees when regarding the fruit trees at the rear of the central panel ? There is a good chance of it. The vision goes on: 'The throne of God and the Lamb will stand there and his servants will honour Him' (Rev 21, 3). In St.John's Gospel, in the conversation with the Samaritan woman, Jesus says: 'Whoever drinks of the (living) water that I shall give him will never thirst; the water that I shall give him will become in him a spring of water welling up to eternal life' (John 4, 14). Further on in the gospel: 'If anyone thirst, let him come to me and drink. He who believes in me, as the scripture has said, 'Out of his heart shall flow rivers of living water' (7, 37).

It is evident that the living water is also associated with the sacrament of baptism. When we then look at the vertical axis of the panel, we see the Holy Ghost, the blood of the sacrificed Lamb and the living water from the fountain. One must here think automatically of the words from the First Letter of John: "There are three witnesses (for Jesus), the Spirit, the water and the blood, and these three correspond." By this John means that both the Spirit of truth and the blood of Christ's self-sacrifice on the Cross and the baptismal water are evidence of the belief in Christ. This illustrates once more the enormous thematic wealth to be found in the retable.

In the background, where the landscape broadens into the blue distance, the horizon is filled with the buildings of the heavenly Jerusalem. It is an imaginary architecture, using Gothic and Rhineland Romanesque styles. Several existing buildings are thought to be identifiable. The tower centre-left may be the Utrecht cathedral tower; Jan Van Eyck also painted it on the panel of the Madonna with Chancellor Rolin (Louvre). The building centre-right, with two short towers, open nave and unfinished choir recalls the state of the cathedral in Cologne at the time, but it is not true to life, since the towers have spires. The tower with the steep spire to the right of it is quite probably the Church of St. Nicholas in Ghent.

The perspective of the landscape fading into blue works better than that of the meadow at the front, which in fact runs too steeply. The meadow still gives a thoroughly two-dimensional impression, but this may have been motivated by the arrangement of the groups of figures against the green background.

To the fore are the groups of the chosen ones from the pre-Christian (A) and the Christian worlds (B).

*Group A*
In group A one sees, at the front, kneeling and with books in their hands, the Old Testament prophets [22]. They form a clearly antithetical symmetry with the kneeling figures in group B. Behind them is a group of largely unidentified characters, probably still a few from the Old Testament, but also heathen figures, of whom it was assumed that they had been saved by their high-principled lives, or had even prepared the way for the coming of Christianity. They come from all over the world, which is suggested by the varied collection of foreign-looking headgear, from turbans to pointed Chinese hats. The characters at the front, robed in red, green and blue may represent the great prophets Isaiah, Jeremiah and Ezechiel (or Daniel?). The figure in blue with the almond branch may certainly be Jeremiah, in whose vision in the Bible there appears an almond branch. But David's father Jesse and the prophet Isaiah are also candidates. The figure dressed in white, with a laurel wreath, is usually identified as the Latin poet Virgil. In the 4th eclogue of his Bucolics the poet sings of the imminent birth of a child that will bring a golden age. In the Christian Middle Ages a prediction of the

Messiah was also read into this. Virgil was highly-regarded, as 'almost' a Christian. It is Virgil that leads the poet Dante through hell and purgatory in his Divine Comedy. One also thinks of teachers, philosophers and monarchs. All these additional identifications inevitably rely on guesswork. This also applies to the other crowd groups in the retable, and one always has to be cautious in this respect, since the involuntary tendency is to look for a well-known figure behind every face.

Despite the great variety in clothing and beards, one notices an undeniable stereotyping of the faces. Among the Apostles in group B this is even clearer. The painter very probably did not want to produce individual portraits, but rather 'typical faces' with certain variations. A number of them may be inspired by traditional images.

The absence of drama, pathos or tension in the faces is again striking. It is difficult to say the characters seem distant, but this group expresses a passion-less introversion and serenity just like the B group. One can hardly speak of any mutual *communio*. The groups help to determine the general atmosphere of the retable.

*Group B*

On the right, in group B, 14 characters are kneeling in the foreground: the 12 Apostles, probably with Paul and Barnabas. It is also thought that Peter (back, 2nd from left, bald), John (in front of Peter, young and clean-shaven, *cf.* the grisaille) and Paul (next to Peter, also almost bald) can be identified. Behind them we see popes, bishops, deacons, all in red robes (indicating martyrdom ?) and in the background prominent non-clerical Christian figures. Their prominence is reflected in their headgear.

Several saints are clearly recognizable from their symbols. Stephen, the first martyr, is dressed in the robe of the deacons, the dalmatic, and in it carries the rocks with which he was stoned to death. The bishop holding his torn-out tongue in tongs may rightly be identified as Livinus, one of the patron saints of Ghent. The three popes have fairly individual facial expressions, and therefore three figures from Van Eyck's time (the so-called great 'Western Schism') have been proposed: Martin V, Alexander V and Gregory XII. Other suggestions have been Gregory the Great, Sixtus III and Sylvester, but all this remains extremely uncertain. The same thing applies to the remaining bishops and abbots.

*Group C*

At the rear two groups approach from between the bushes, also to honour the Lamb. On the left (C) the group of saints known as the 'confessors', meaning that they did not acquire their sainthood as martyrs. Blue robes and white albs dominate the colour palette in this group. The monarchs carry the palm of victory in their hands. At the front one recognizes three popes and a group of cardinals, bishops and abbots, but none of the figures has special accessories, so additional identifications are impossible.

*Group D*

On the right (D) the holy women approach, virgins and martyrs, all carrying the palm of victory in the hand and their heads covered by wreaths. Several of

them are recognizable by means of their traditional symbols: Saint Agnes with her Lamb, Saint Barbara with the tower and Saint Dorothy with a basket of flowers. The saint holding an arrow in her hand could be Ursula; the princess in an ermine robe is very probably Saint Catherine of Alexandria, even though she is shown without her wheel. In addition one sees several abbesses with their croziers.

Shining over the whole of this scene is the dove in a gleaming three-part aureole: the Holy Ghost. The light coming from this image has an exceptionally strong pictorial effect on the whole composition. The motif of the semicircular aureole, divided into rings, is reminiscent of what one often sees in mosaics and frescos covering the vaults of niches in the apses of basilicas and Romanesque churches. God's hand is shown, surrounded by a semicircle comprising

concentric rings of colour, which suggest heaven. But here the 'light of the Holy Ghost' achieves much more than its theologically symbolic value: it is not only the heavenly Jerusalem on which the light of God's spirit shines, but the whole panel, which is illuminated by this luminous halo in the blue sky, whose fine golden rays reach to the front and which divides into balanced segments the symmetrical cohesion of the whole.

### Panels 8, 9, 11 and 12

The panels 8,9,11,12 are given a separate setting and perspective, but in terms of composition may be considered as an extension of the central scene. On the four side panels we see the members of various groups who are on their way to join the crowds of chosen ones in the meadow. One might think of a classification into those who are 'of the world', and there bear responsibility: the Just Judges and the Knights of Christ, and those who 'have left the world': the repentant sinners and hermits, and the pilgrims.

Panel 8 depicts the *Iusti Iudices* - the Just Judges. They are judges whose irreproachable lives have allowed them to enter the glory of heaven. A large number of identifications had been ventured even before the authentic panel was replaced by the copy. They thought of both ruling lords and Ghent magistrates[23]. None of these identifications can be proved, and caution is advised. The present panel is a copy by J. van der Veken, painted in 1939-40 to replace the stolen original. It is a very clever copy, but the differences in colours are noticeable (see, for example, the sky and the rocks) as is the much flatter execution, of the horses, for example. It is said that Van der Veken gave to one of the riders (back, 2nd from left, with red hat) the facial features of the then monarch, King Leopold III of Belgium.

On panel 9 nine riders are depicted, knights and princes, who bear the name *Cristi Milites* - 'the Knights of Christ'. The princes are preceded by three laurelled young knights with ceremonial harnesses and pennants. Because of their number it has been thought that the legendary *neuf preux* were depicted: Joshua, David and Judas Maccabeus from the Old Testament, Hector, Alexander and Julius Caesar from classical antiquity, and King Arthur, Charlemagne and Godfrey of Bouillon from the medieval period. One might venture to make individual identifications of Charlemagne (at the back with a clasped crown) and the crusader Godfrey of Bouillon (riding a mule?). But there is no certainty. People have also thought about the Saints Michael, Victor, George and about Jean de Berry, Sigismund of Luxemburg, Louis IX of France and others. Once again, one must not overestimate the worth of these designations.

Panel 11 takes us into a completely different world: the *Heremitae Sancti* - Holy Hermits. In their case there are no buildings in the background, as for the judges and knights: they live far away from the inhabited world, amongst rocks, trees and bushes. Because of the rather high horizon the background looks a little crowded, but the green and brown colouring provides a rare richness. The middle figure, with rosary and staff, bears a T on his shirt. This allows us to identify him with the Holy Hermit Anthony. In the background we recognize the repentant Mary Magdalen, who carries her symbol, the pot of ointment with which she had anointed Christ. Next to her is an unidentified female companion.

Panel 12 shows the *Peregrini Sancti* - the Holy Pilgrims. Note the impressively beautiful Mediterranean landscape through which they are walking, and which demonstrates a great continuity with the adjacent panel. The vegetation is reproduced with astonishing subtlety on both panels. The pilgrims are led by the giant, red-robed figure of Christopher. According to legend, the patron saint of travellers was in fact a giant. The pilgrim next to St. Christopher is carrying the shell of St.James of Compostela on his pilgrim's hood, and may probably be identified with St. Judocus, patron saint of the commissioner of the retable.

13: The prophet Zachariah (Zacharias).
14: The Sibyl of Eritrea.
15: The Sibyl of Cumae.
16: The prophet Micah (Micheas).
17: The angel Gabriel brings the message to Mary.
18: Interior: view out into a street in Ghent.
19: Interior: washbasin with towel.
20: Mary in prayer, overshadowed by the Holy Ghost.
21: Judocus Vijd, donor of the retable.
22: John the Baptist.
23: John the Evangelist.
24: Isabella Borluut, wife of the donor. [14]

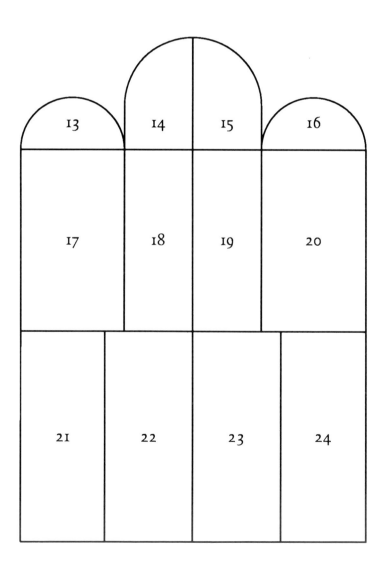

On the closed retable one can also see two clearly distinguishable levels. The upper can be linked to the story of salvation pictured on the open retable. The lower, one might call the official presentation of the work of art and the motivation for its execution. We shall take the upper level first.

UPPER LEVEL

*Panels 17,18,19 and 20*
The panels 17,18,19,20 form a definite whole: the message of the angel Gabriel to Mary. This scene is taken from St. Luke's Gospel, and in the Christian tradition and liturgy forms the beginning of the events revolving around the birth of Jesus. Thematically speaking, this scene should be inserted between Adam and Eve's sin and the redemption by means of Christ's crucifixion, the sacrifice of the Lamb. The church says that deliverance was set in motion when Christ was born as a man.

What is striking is the enormous difference in colouring between the open and the closed retable. The colours on the open retable are gleaming, clear, festive, often with the effect of shining metal; those on the closed retable are discreet, more monochrome, more subdued. The main accent here is given by brown, beige and cream (sandstone) tints. It is only the portraits of the donors that contrast with this, in red and green, but these are much softer than the reds and greens on the open retable. The retable was only opened on Sundays and religious holidays; it was the closed retable that provided the daily view. It is as if the colours are also intended to express this difference between the everyday and the festive. But even so, what richness and warmth radiates from the brown and sandstone palette of the closed retable.

The angel Gabriel appears on panel 17, sent from God to request Mary's cooperation in the salvation plan. He is carrying the lily, symbol of Mary's virginity. Symmetrically placed opposite him, kneeling on an open book, is Mary, overshadowed by the Holy Ghost. Note how the dialogue between the two is portrayed: the angel's words of greeting *Ave gracia plena D[omi]n[u]s Tecu[m]* - 'greetings, full of grace, the Lord is with you' stand upright; Mary's answer, *Ecce ancilla d[omi]ni* - 'see the Lord's handmaiden' was painted upside

It is precisely the modesty of the objects depicted that plays a substantial part in the creation of the atmosphere of the Annunciation scene. There is much more going on, however. Beyond his masterly still-life technique, (Jan?) Van Eyck reveals himself to be a master of pictorial abstraction. The towel next to the washbasin forms a simple white rectangle. This bright white in the centre of the closed section acts almost as a source of light and creates a striking effect, connecting up the surrounding figures. When one covers this white area on a reproduction, the difference is startling. However realistically the towel may be reproduced, one must never forget that the painter is not making a documentary on the interior in Nazareth! He has total freedom in the choice and positioning of his objects, and in doing so allows himself to be guided by pictorial strength. Strictly speaking, Van Eyck could have put a window there, or shown a piece of green tapestry… The choice of white, in a geometric form and close to the centre indicates exactly the pictorial function of the area of colour as something abstract. It is not important that a towel is hanging next to a washbasin. It is important that a white area distributes the light in the closed retable.

65

down, and runs from right to left - so back in the direction of the angel. The whole scene is traditionally taken from the beginning of St.Luke's Gospel, where the birth of the Messiah is heralded in this way. The setting of the angel's message at the time of Mary's prayers is completely traditional. It provides the scene with the character of a sort of mystical experience for the madonna.

Behind Mary there is a small space, a sort of vaulted room. It gives the scene additional depth. The same space is also suggested behind the angel, but less pronouncedly. In the furthest wall of both rooms a glassless window looks out on the small town of Nazareth, where the Annunciation takes place. The two windows, with an unnoticeably altered perspective, are linked by the panels 18 and 19, an exceptionally atmospheric interior of a room. Something noteworthy is going on here, which once more proves how much Van Eyck is concerned with pictorial composition and not documentary photography. In the two central panels the wall has been shifted forwards, and in such a way that, for those who are keen on realism, it seems as if there is no entrance anywhere to the rooms behind. Indeed, the low wall below and the ceiling beams run unbroken through the four panels. There might be an indication, in this way of working, of a change in the original concept. Whatever is the case, the shift in the arrangement of space, for pictorial reasons, is conspicuous.

Panel 19 again dumbfounds us with Van Eyck's versatility. We see an incredibly lovely still-life, which fills the upper level daringly but without a trace of anecdotalism. As has been stated, anecdotal interest is entirely foreign to Van Eyck in this retable.

One notices another still-life on the right next to Mary's head: a niche in the wall with several objects, a copper candlestick and water jug, a small pottery vase, two books. How movingly Van Eyck fills with life these silent witnesses to the Annunciation!

Panel 18 depicts a street in the city. The question has rightly been asked here whether this is a reproduction of an existing medieval town, or, to be more precise, Ghent. On the basis of the possible identification of several buildings, attention has often been focused on the Korte Dagsteeg in Ghent, looking towards the Walpoort. Taking this further, the suggestion was made that Van Eyck simply painted the view from his studio. If this were true, we would have a valuable indication of the site of his studio: on the corner of the present-day Vogelmarkt and Koestraat, looking along the Korte Dagsteeg. The corner house currently situated there does indeed bear a medallion portraying the Van Eyck brothers, in reference to the town view in the Adoration of the Lamb.

At the top are the panels 13 to 16. They are the most closely linked to the Annunciation scene. It is part of the oldest Christian tradition that the coming of the Messiah, who was to save his people, was predicted in a mysterious way. The New Testament writers had themselves read the prediction in various prophecies in the Old Testament. But when the Christian faith came into contact with the heathens, people started to believe that the coming of Christ had also been predicted by heathen seers. In the proclamation section, Van Eyck reproduced two Biblical and two heathen predictions. In the semicircular lunettes we see the prophets Zachariah on the left and Micah on the

Van Eyck apparently occupied himself a great deal with the study of perspective and three-dimensionality. In this retable he tried them out several times in 'trompe l'oeil' effects. Adam's foot is one example, but a very fine one is the book held by the prophet Micah, which extends over the edge of the frame. It is as though Micah is watching from a balcony the fulfilment of his prophecy in Mary's room.

right. On the Latin banderoles there are texts concerning the coming of the Messiah [24]. From heathenism one sees, in the middle, two heathen prophetesses called sibyls. According to tradition they had also foretold the coming of Christ. On the left, in white robes, the Sibyl of Eritrea; on the right the Sibyl of Cumae. On their scrolls there are rather puzzling texts, which nevertheless concern the Annunciation [25]. The universality expressed here is striking: the sibyls are heathen prophetesses, and heathens even appear in heaven on Van Eyck's inner panel.

LOWER LEVEL

*Panels 21 and 24*
on the sections 21 and 24 Van Eyck has portrayed the donors of the polyptych in prayer. It is thought that these portraits of Judocus Vijd and Isabella Borluut may be attributed to Jan Van Eyck. This motif is traditional. On most medieval retables the praying donors take part in the scene depicted. It is as if they were directly involved in it. One only has to think of two other works by Van Eyck: the 'Virgin Mary with Chancellor Rolin' in the Louvre and the 'Virgin with Canon Van der Paele' in the Groeninghe Museum in Bruges. In the much more complex and compartmentalized composition of the Adoration of the Lamb, the donors are more isolated. They do not participate directly in the Adoration of the Lamb on the inner section, but are given their place under the Annunciation scene. Their pictorial framing is a work of genius, however: above and to the side they are bordered by the cloaks of Mary and the angel, and of both the pictures of John. This beige and sandstone-coloured 'mass' forms a marvellous counterpoint to the robes and gives the deep red a very special delicate and warm tonality. A brainwave like this, in colour composition, helps to prove how much of a master of abstraction Van Eyck was, for whom the primary concern was forms and areas of colour. Imagine a modern abstract painting in which the panels of the angel and Mary and the two pictures of the saints were plain beige and sandstone-coloured areas, and where the donors would also be replaced by red areas. It would give a more direct impression of the influence of colour framing, because nothing figurative would be involved. But what Van

Eyck has in mind is essentially the same. Imagine for a moment how different the red of the donors would look if the framing were multicoloured, or blue, or black[26].

Both portraits belong among the flawless examples of the Flemish school, but display that approach which is Van Eyck's unmistakable signature: with his relentless powers of observation, the painter penetrates into the marrow of the inner man. Just think of Canon Van der Paele, Chancellor Rolin, the man with the red turban (a self-portrait?) or Van Eyck's own wife Margareta. There is no notion of friendly, flattering superficiality or idealization. This is the case here too: both figures radiate seriousness, distinction and serenity. But also intelligence and will-power - I also see a certain cunning and calculation in the face of Joos Vijd, and something unidentified bottled up in Isabella... Their clothing reflects their social status and discrete wealth. There is a tradition that Albrecht Dürer was inspired by the praying hands in the Ghent retable when executing his famous 'Praying Hands'.

*Middle panels 22 and 23*
Finally, the lower middle sections 22 and 23 contain the pictures of the two saints who were most closely involved in the creation of the Adoration of the Lamb. On the left the patron saint of the Church of St.John, John the Baptist. The Church of St.John was only given the name of St.Bavo's in 1540, when St.Bavo's Abbey was dismantled by Charles the Fifth as a punishment, in order to make way for a citadel, the so-called Spanish Castle. The emperor wished to use this to keep the rebellious city of his birth under restraint. The chapter of St.Bavo's Abbey was then transferred to the Church of St.John, which from then on became the Church, and from 1559 the Cathedral, of St.Bavo. The crypt in St.Bavo's is still dedicated to St.John the Baptist, however. The right-hand image is that of St.John the Evangelist, who is traditionally not only considered to be the author of the Gospel of St.John, but also of the Book of Revelation, from which the main subject of the retable was taken.

Both images provide perfect examples of imitational painting in grisaille, although the colour is not grey, but sandstone, which gives a greater warmth to the images. While St.John the Baptist is carrying a Lamb as emblem, St.John the Evangelist is holding a goblet of writhing adders. This emblem reminds us of a legend that tells how a priest at the temple of Artemis (Diana) in Ephesus challenged John to drink a poisoned cup, which he did, without ill effects.

The four figures in the lower section were all placed in a sandstone niche, whose decoration comprises two slender columns above which a trilobate Gothic arch rises, with stylized flower patterns in the corners. The rear wall behind the donors is flat and behind the saints takes the form of an apse. The angle of light and shadow creates the perfect illusion of being formed by the real light shining in through the stained-glass window opposite in the Vijd Chapel, as it does in the upper section.

In this way the donors and the patron saints today still present the eternal masterpiece whose existence they made possible.

The portrait of Isabella Borluut reminds us a lot of that of Margareta van Eyck, Jan's wife. The fashions of the time will have something to do with it. But the white of the hood and the green of the folded sleeve break the too rigid symmetrical arrangement with respect to Joos Vijd and strongly emphasize the praying hands.

The Sibyl of Eritrea (now on the West coast of Turkey) was given a more exotic touch: heavy lips and a voluminous turban. How splendidly the large blue and white surface contrasts with the black collar, and she fills the narrow space, which is, so to speak, made broader.

# Notes

1 This is not absolutely certain. The gravestone is currently in the Romanesque refectory of St. Bavo's Abbey. It is damaged and it is no longer possible to attribute it precisely. But it does correspond extraordinarily well to a description of Hubert's gravestone written by the Ghent chronicler Marcus van Vaernewijck in 1568.

2 E.Dhanens, *Hubert en Jan Van Eyck (Hubert and Jan Van Eyck)*, Mercatorfonds, 1980, p.7.

3 There was much discussion on the authenticity and value of this quatrain. We cannot go into this discussion, but take up the position currently held by most specialists, who accept that the information in the verse corresponds to the reality. On the same day Philip the Good and Isabella of Portugal's son, Joos (the same name as Joos Vijd!) was born in the Prinsenhof in Ghent and baptized in the Church of St.John.

4 The most well-known member of the family was Jan Borluut, leader of a contingent of Ghent people during the Battle of the Spurs on 11th July 1302, when the Flemish militias defeated Philip the Fair's French army of knights.

5 Entering the southern choir aisle from the steps in the transept, it is the 6th chapel. A wooden frame indicates the original position of the retable. The windows in the Vijd Chapel are recent and were made by H.Blondeel to commemorate the 25th jubilee of Mgr.L.A.Van Peteghem, 28th Bishop of Ghent.

6 The term 'New Testament' means the holy scriptures of the Christian church. There are 27 scriptures, all of which concern Christ in one way or another and contain the heart of the Christian message. There are four gospels, attributed to Matthew, Mark, Luke and John, all of which deal with Jesus' words and deeds, but especially with his suffering, death and resurrection. The gospels are followed by a book about the earliest history of the church, written by Luke. This book is called the 'Acts of the Apostles' and tells mainly of the birth of the church in Jerusalem and the spread of the religion among the gentiles by the actions of the apostle Paul. There are, in addition, 21 letters, of which 14 are traditionally attributed to the apostle Paul, 1 to James, 2 to Peter, 3 to John and 1 to the apostle Jude. Finally there is the Book of Revelation or Apocalypse, attributed to John, from which the subject of the Van Eycks' retable was derived.

7 One remarkable thing is that the lamb on Van Eyck's altar looks like an adult sheep, which cannot be accidental for someone of Van Eyck's powers of observation. Paschal lambs are, by definition, newborn, since Passover takes place at the time when the young are being born. Is it just that the artist bases his representation on the idea of an *adult* crucified Christ?

8 A.L.Dierick, *Van Eyck. The Adoration of the Lamb,*

Ghent, 1972, pp.4v.

9 Pim Brinkman, *Het geheim van Van Eyck. Aantekeningen bij de uitvinding van het olieverven (The mystery of Van Eyck. Notes concerning the invention of oil painting)*, Zwolle, Waanders, 1993, 347pp.

10 A.De Kegel, *De Sint-Baafskathedraal van Gent. Een kunstkamer. (St.Bavo's Cathedral in Ghent. An art treasury)*, in Art in Public Possession in Flanders, 30 (1992), 1, p.30.

11 We derive this from A.L.Dierick, *Van Eyck. The Adoration of the Lamb*, p.22.

12 Quoted in: E.Dhanens, *op.cit.* p.78.91.

13 Cf.Id., *Ibid.*, p.91.

14 For the description of the panels we follow the excellent guide by R.Van De Wielle, *De Sint-Baafskathedraal te Gent (St.Bavo's Cathedral in Ghent)*, 1988, p.42. For the numbering of the outer sections, however, we use the order that corresponds to the closed retable, and not to the present open position.

15 A strong case is made for this by L.Dequeker, *Joodse exegese op het Lam-Godsretabel in de Sint-Baafskathedraal te Gent (Jewish exegesis in the Adoration of the Lamb retable in St.Bavo's Cathedral in Ghent)*, in: C.Verdegaal, W.Weren (ed.), *Stromen uit Eden (Currents from Eden)*, Boxtel-Brugge, 1992.

16 See Gen 49,10; Num 24,17 and others: texts like this were regularly applied to Christ in Christian tradition.

17 See Isaiah 6, 3.

18 We find a striking illustration of the problem in the publications of Dr. Elisabeth Dhanens. In her *Retable of the Adoration of the Lamb in St.Bavo's Cathedral in Ghent*, 1965, this art history specialist argues strongly for identifying the enthroned figure as the Father. In her great monograph on *Hubert en Jan Van Eyck*, 1980, she opts unequivocally for Christ. The difficulty is also illustrated in other places on the retable. On panel 9 we see a red transverse band running over the shield of the middle 'Knight of Christ'. There is a text displayed on this band. On the vertical band we read DS (= Deus, God) FORTIS ADONAJ SABAOT V(ae?): Powerful God, Lord of Hosts. On the horizontal band: EMA//EL IHS T XRC AGLA: Emmanuel Jesus T Christ AGLA. For the meaning of AGLA, see the inscription in the picture of the tiled floors with the musical angels. The T is in the centre of the shield and connects the vertical and horizontal bands. The T, the Greek letter Tau, is a symbol of Christ's cross. The knight is also a Knight of Christ. This may mean that the entire text on the shield actually refers to Christ. In the case of the horizontal band this is clear, but the titles on the vertical band, which are also partly to be found on the representation of the Almighty, might make us think of God the father. To me it seems that the text on the shield indicates that all the writings apply to Christ, and therefore also

the words "Deus, Adonai and Sabaoth". But strictly speaking it may be a mixing of symbols for Father and Son.

19 John 1, 36v.

20 'Deutero-Isaiah' means 'second Isaiah' and is the academic name for an anonymous prophet, who lived in the 6th century BC and made his appearance during the Jewish exile in Babylon. The writings of this prophet were added to the book of Isaiah and cover chapters 40 to 55.

21 Like everywhere in the Bible, twelve is the number symbolic of fullness and perfection. The association with the twelve tribes of Israel, the chosen people, is never far away.

22 Although only 11 figures can be counted in this first group, they have often been called the 12 'small prophets' of the Old Testament. The four great ones are behind them. The white figure, generally accepted to be Virgil, has therefore also been equated with Ezechiel.

23 It was thought that Van Eyck had portrayed a number of Dukes of Flanders: Philip the Bold, John the Fearless, Philip the Good, Louis of Male. Jean de Berry, William IV of Bavaria, the Byzantine emperor John IV Paleologus, Henry V of England and others have also been named. It was even thought that Jan Van Eyck had portrayed himself in the group.

24 For Zachariah: 'cheer loudly, daughter of Sion (= Jerusalem), rejoice, because look, your king is coming' (Zach 9,9). For Micah: 'Out of you will spring the one who shall be lord of Israel' (Mic 5,2).

25 The sibyls were very well-known in the Christian Middle Ages. The sibyl is also mentioned in the famous *Dies Irae* from the Latin Requiem mass. *Dies irae dies illa solvet saeclum in favilla, teste David cum Sibylla*. The Sibyl of Eritrea's banderole contains a text from Virgil's Aeneid (Aen VI,vv.50-51). The text says: 'You speak no human tongue, inspired as it is by the force from on high'. That of Cumae contains - wrongly, in fact - a prophecy attributed in reality to the Sibyl of Eritrea, and is taken from the work *De Civitate Dei* - The City of God, by St. Augustine. The text says: 'The highermost king will come in human form to rule across the centuries.'

26 Perhaps it is here that we come across the most important shortcoming in the present-day setting of the polyptych. Since it is permanently open, one can only see the closed part at the back, without distance in which to view it. The figures are separated from each other by a broad black partition, and have their backs to each other. It demands a great effort from the spectator to reconstruct in his mind the unity of the composition and in particular the superb arrangement of the colours. Fortunately this problem has been partially solved by a smaller model which *can* be closed.

# Concise list of literature consulted

- CELS, Jos, *De Roof van de Rechtvaardige Rechters. Geschiedenis van de opzienbarende kunstroof in de Sint-Baafskathedraal te Gent*, 4th imp. Antwerpen-Bussum, 1983, 173 pp.
- COREMANS, P. - JANSSENS DE BISTHOVEN, A., *Van Eyck. L'adoration de l'Agneau Mystique* ACIAN, Primitifs Flamands, vol. 1. Eng. Trans. (M. Davies) *The Adoration of the Mystic Lamb*, Amsterdam - Antwerp, 1948, 45 pp. + 209 pp.ill.
- DE BAETS, J., *De gewijde teksten van "Het Lam Gods" retabel. Kritisch onderzocht*, s.l. (Maldegem), s.d. (1984), 88 pp.
- DEQUEKER, Luc, *Joodse exegese in het Lam-Godsretabel in de Sint-Baafskathedraal te Gent*, in: C. Verdegaal - W. Weren (ed.), *Stromen uit Eden*, Boxtel-Brugge, 1992, pp. 195-211.
- DHANENS, Elisabeth, *De Patriciërs en het Lam Godsretabel*, in: Firmin De Smidt - Elisabeth Dhanens, *De Sint-Baafskathedraal te Gent*, Tielt, 1980, pp. 152-176.
- DHANENS, Elisabeth, *Het retabel van het Lam Gods in de Sint-Baafskathedraal te Gent. Inventaris van het kunstpatrimonium van Oostvlaanderen*, VI, Ghent, 1965, 121 pp. ill.
- DHANENS, Elisabeth, *Hubert en Jan Van Eyck*, Antwerp, Mercatorfonds, 1980, Ill.
- DIERICK, Alfons L., *Van Eyck. Het Lam Gods*, Ghent, 1972, 48 pp. Ill.
- DIERICK, Alfons L., *Joos Vijds Tafele. De retabel van het Lam Gods. Van Eycks meesterwerk in kleuren en op ware grootte*, Ghent, Dierick, 1995, 88 pp. III
- HEYMANS, H., "Hier sagh men schilders jong en oudt en alle constbeminders omtrent swermen", in: Ram-Rapport 4, Maaseik, 1990, 65-86. Ill.
- KEGEL, Andrea De, *Het Lam Godsretabel door Jan en Hubrecht van Eyck*, in: *De Sint-Baafskathedraal van Gent. Een kunstkamer* (ed. Geert van Doorne), Openbaar Kunstbezit in Vlaanderen, 1992,1, 24-32, Ill.
- MORTIER, Karel - KERCKHAERT, Noël, *De Rechtvaardige Rechters gestolen. Een kriminologische studie*. Ghent, 1968, XLVIII-276 pp. Ill.
- MORTIER, Karel - KERCKHAERT, Noël, *Dossier Lam Gods. Zoektocht naar De Rechtvaardige Rechters*, Ghent, 1994, 579 + 85 pp. Ill.
- PINET, André, *Het Lam Gods*, Paris-Antwerp, 1987, 64 pp. Ill.
- PUYVELDE, Leo Van, *L'agneau Mystique*, Brussels, 1946, 125 pp. Ill. (Ned. vert. *Het Lam Gods*, Rotterdam, 1948, 125 pp. Ill.)
- STEPPE, J.K., *De echo van het "Lam Gods" van de gebroeders Van Eyck in Spanje*, in: Ram-Rapport 4, Maaseik, 1990, 3-63. Ill.

# Contents

Schmidt, Peter
The Adoration of the Lamb

Leuven, Davidsfonds, 1995
Blijde-Inkomststraat 79-81, 3000 Leuven
80 pages
© 1995, Publishing House Davidsfonds/Leuven
Printed and bound by Drukkerij Lannoo NV, Tielt

Design: Gregie de Maeyer
Photo's: Paul Maeyaert
Advice on choice of illustrations: Paul Maeyaert
Translator: Gregory Ball

D/1995/0240/3
ISBN 90-6152-876 3